Bro.

insp

you to always serve the interests of Jesus in the love of the Holy Family Thanks for your suggestions in the text.

The Holy Spouses Rosary

Fr. Larry Toschi, O.S.J.

Fr. Larry, O.S.J.

To DAVE, KATIE, & FAMILY.

I HELPED CORRECT & EDIT THIS; BUT IT IS THE PROJECT OF ONE OF MY EX-SUPERIORS,

Guardian of the Redeemer Publications
544 West Cliff Dr.
Santa Cruz, CA 95060

http://osjoseph.org

MAY ITS PRAYER BRING YOUR FAMILY BLESSINGS

WELCOME HOME,
JOE STARKWEATHER 8-20-21

Cum permissu superiorum
Fr. John Warburton, O.S.J., Provincial
Oblates of St. Joseph, California Province
December 30, 2011, Feast of the Holy Family

Nihil obstat
Msgr. James Peterson, censor librorum
Diocese of Fresno
January 18, 2012

Imprimatur
Msgr. Myron Cotta, Diocesan Administrator
Diocese of Fresno
January 23, 2012, Feast of the Holy Spouses

Library of Congress Control Number: 2013933967
Toschi, Larry M.
The Holy Spouses Rosary – 1st ed. 2013
ISBN 978-1-883839-08-6
St. Joseph, Mary, Holy Spouses, Rosary, Marriage, Chastity

Thanks to: Michele and Thomas Spencer, and Bro. Joseph Starkweather, O.S.J. for reviewing the text and offering helpful suggestions; Oblates of St. Joseph from various countries for translations into their languages.

Dedicated to

Fr. Tarcisio Stramare, O.S.J.

*whose lifelong writings provide the
foundation for many of the reflections contained herein
(which nevertheless remain the responsibility of the author)*

Contents

Introduction

*T*he purpose of this book and the devotion presented herein is to allow you to focus on Christ through the lens of the two people who were closest to him on earth and who remain closest to him in heaven. The Holy Spouses, Mary and Joseph, received the Incarnate Son of God into their marriage, nurtured and raised him together, formed the Holy Family with him, and for many years did their part to help prepare him for his saving mission. They are the greatest models of Christian living and the most powerful intercessors. Reflection on their participation in the redemptive mysteries of Christ's hidden life is a sure aid to holiness in our ordinary, everyday lives.

What is the Holy Spouses Rosary?

The Holy Spouses Rosary is based upon the venerable, time-tried, and officially approved devotion known as the Marian Rosary. It complements and extends this devotion in a way that includes Saint Joseph, Mary's husband and Jesus' earthly (though not biological) father. It is prayed using the same beads, but the "Hail Mary" is substituted by a prayer patterned after it in a way that includes Joseph and is thus directed to the "Holy Spouses" together, rather than to Mary alone. While not a direct part of the Luminous, Sorrowful, or Glorious mysteries, St. Joseph is an integral part of proper reflection on the Joyful mysteries, which are here extended from five to ten in the Holy Spouses Mysteries of the Incarnation and the Hidden Life.

Why is Saint Joseph important for the rosary?

The connection is not totally new. In 1889 Pope Leo XIII issued an encyclical on devotion to St. Joseph, linking it directly to devotion to Mary and providing a particular prayer to be prayed always at the end of the rosary: "To you, O Blessed Joseph,…"[1] A century later Blessed Pope John Paul II repeated this request in his own apostolic exhortation on the Guardian of the Redeemer.[2] In a subsequent apostolic letter on the Rosary of the Virgin Mary, the same pope tied the rosary to the renewal of the family, so threatened in our times.[3] He also referred to "the home of Nazareth" and stated that by "seeing the household of Nazareth, [believers] learn the original truth of the family according to God's plan," and the sanctity of life.[4] Without mentioning St. Joseph, such references to family and household certainly presume his presence.

By extending many of the thoughts in this apostolic letter of Blessed John Paul II, we may find a solid grounding for the Holy Spouses Rosary. Most of what he says about Mary has implications for Joseph, her husband. Who was more devoted to Mary than Joseph? He leads us more deeply into Marian devotion. Moreover, together these Holy Spouses are teachers at whose school we learn "to contemplate the beauty on the face of Christ and to experience the depth of his love."[5] This devotion is totally Christ-centered, as were their lives.

Mary and Joseph are models of contemplation, marveling together at the Son of God from the womb unto adulthood. Think of their wonder gazing into each other's eyes after the news of the Incarnation. Ponder their look beholding the face of their newborn at Bethlehem. Picture how "his father and his mother marveled at what was said about him" as holy Simeon took him in his arms (Lk 2:25-33). Feel their pain to think that hateful Herod sought to kill the innocent face of love in which they found such delight. Visualize their questioning expression during the episode of the finding in the Temple: "Son, why have you treated us so?" (Lk 2:48).[6] Imagine their untold moments raising Jesus, conversing with him, praying with him, working with him, and simply watching him grow in wisdom, age, and grace before their eyes. By together contemplating God Incarnate, Mary and Joseph shared a bond that no one else could ever match.

Praying with the Holy Spouses draws us together to wonder at the same mysteries of which they were such an integral part. The Holy Spouses Rosary is a contemplative prayer that starts with the experience of Mary and Joseph. Its "quiet rhythm and lingering pace"[7] helps us meditate on the mysteries of the Lord's infancy and youth as seen through the eyes of the two people who were closest to him. Reflection on the hidden life of Christ, prior to his public ministry, enables us not only to learn about Christ's words and deeds, but first of all to "learn Christ."[8] No one can acquaint us with him better than the Holy Spouses.

By entering into familiar conversation with Jesus, Mary, and Joseph, and by meditating on the mysteries of the Holy Spouses Rosary and living in communion with the Holy Family, we can learn to imitate these supreme models "of humility, poverty, hiddenness, patience, and perfection."[9]

In this process of being conformed to Christ, we entrust ourselves to Mary, Mother of the Church, and Joseph, Patron of the Church. As the Holy Spouses fulfilled the rites of circumcision and naming for the infant Jesus, so do they nurture new members of the mystical body of Christ. As they watched over the human growth of Jesus in their home at Nazareth, so do they teach and shape us with care, until Christ is "fully formed" in us (Gal 4:19). In the Holy Spouses Rosary we go to and pray with the two most powerful intercessors of all times.[10]

At the center of redemption, for the coming of his Son into the world, God placed a couple, Mary and Joseph, to replace our sinful first parents, Adam and Eve. Whereas great and important efforts have always been made to defend the virginity of Mary, we must not think of her or approach her as an unmarried woman. It is equally important to defend the authenticity of the marriage of the Holy Spouses.[11] In them marriage is purified and sanctified. The spousal gift of self is most fully realized in their virginity. A new sacramental reality is established. They actively participate in the work of salvation on earth and in eternity. The marriage of Mary and Joseph is a symbol of the Church, which like Christ is virgin and spouse.[12] "What God has joined no one must separate" (Mt 19:6).

Inclusion of Joseph together with Mary in the mysteries of Christ's infancy is most important for full comprehension of God's unfathomable love. "Christ's whole life is a mystery of redemption," which is at work also in his Incarnation and his years of hidden life.[13] The Joyful Mysteries of the Marian Rosary are most fittingly completed by the Mysteries of the Holy Spouses Rosary. The Holy Spouses are most important models and intercessors for couples, for families, and for every Christian believer.

The Holy Spouses Prayer

The Holy Spouses prayer, repeated ten times for each mystery, is patterned after the "Hail, Mary." It opens with the two titles with which the angel addresses Mary and Joseph at their respective annunciations: "Mary, full of grace, and Joseph, son of David" (Lk 1:28, Mt 1:20). Next, the Church's time-honored title for Mary, "Mother of God," is complemented by the Church's more recent choice of title for Joseph, "guardian of the Redeemer."[14] While Mary and Joseph are honored, the child Jesus is eternally praised: he is the center of their family, and his name remains at the very center of this prayer, as it should for every prayer. Mary and Joseph are invoked together as "Holy Spouses" and their prayers are sought not simply for ourselves as individuals, but also for our families and communities. The prayer is:

> *Mary, full of grace, and Joseph, son of David; honor to you, Mother of God, and to you, guardian of the Redeemer. Eternal praise to the child with whom you formed a family, Jesus.*
>
> Holy Spouses, pray for us sinners, our families and communities, now and at the hour of our death. Amen.

Bringing together the two annunciations to Mary and Joseph and their common role of parenting and raising Jesus, the words of this prayer provide a background for the events of the coming of the Messiah into the world and for his years of hidden preparation for his public ministry. Jesus is clearly the object of these annunciations and of this attentive upbringing. The prayer puts us into living communion with Jesus through the love of his mother and earthly father.[15]

The Mysteries of the Incarnation and Hidden Life

Everything in Jesus' life was a sign of the mystery of redemption. His humanity appeared as a sacrament of his divinity and of the salvation he brings.[16] God's love is manifest in "Christ's whole earthly life – his words and deeds, his silences and sufferings, indeed his manner of being and speaking."[17] The mystery of redemption that culminates in the cross was prepared for in advance by God's providence. It was at work in Jesus' entire life, including the mysteries of his infancy and hidden life.[18] The paschal mystery of his dying and rising was already present in the sorrows and joys that he experienced in the presence of Mary and Joseph. More than anyone else the Holy Spouses help us gaze upon the mysteries of the first 30 years of the life of the Redeemer.

It is likely that Mary and Joseph alone shared the secret of the virginal conception of Jesus,[19] a secret that is never mentioned throughout the public ministry. Even though Jesus clearly proclaims himself the Son of God, nowhere is it recorded that he revealed the manner of his Incarnation. He was presumed to be the son of Joseph[20] through the normal manner of conception. It is likely that Mary would not feel free to reveal the mystery of conception by the Holy Spirit to anyone except Joseph, who accepted her word through faith and subsequently had his own annunciation confirming that word. Only after the resurrection, the ascension, and the coming of the same Holy Spirit upon the apostles at Pentecost, would Mary share this mystery with the apostles. This would be the source for the virginal conception being reported in the infancy narratives of the Gospels of Matthew and Luke, and nowhere else in the New Testament. Mary and Joseph therefore provide the only lens through which to view firsthand the mysteries of the Incarnation and hidden life of the Son of God.

The litany-like succession of the Holy Spouses prayer becomes "an unceasing praise of Christ,"[21] who is the providential reason for their betrothal, the object of their respective annunciations, and the center of their lives through their shared experience of his birth and growth. More completely than the traditional five joyful mysteries of the rosary, the following ten mysteries of the Holy Spouses Rosary prepare us for the relatively new luminous mysteries, and the traditional sorrowful and glorious mysteries of the Marian rosary, in which Joseph is no longer present. For the Holy Spouses Rosary, the Mysteries of the Incarnation and Hidden Life are as follows:

1. *The Betrothal* (Mt 1:18a, Lk 1:26-27, 2:4-5a). Before the Incarnation the immaculate virgin and the just man are wedded to each other in true married love. The mystery of the Savior's coming into the world begins with a betrothed couple whose relationship is based upon a desire to give themselves entirely to God's love. In ways they could not know, this betrothal "was part of the very plan of God."[22]

2. *The Annunciation to Mary* (Lk 1:28-38). God chooses the virgin Mary, betrothed to Joseph of the house of David, for the miracle of his coming in human flesh. The Son of God becomes dependant on acceptance by a human mother, and thereupon takes the nature of a tiny being in her womb.

3. *The Annunciation to Joseph* (Mt 1:18b-23). God's design is for Mary's husband, the just man of the house of David, to continue with their plans to form a home together, and to name and act as father to the child conceived by the Holy Spirit.

4. *Joseph Takes Mary his Wife into his Home* (Mt 1:24-25). The Son of God depends upon a chosen human father, committed in a virginal marriage, to provide a loving, caring, and wholesome home for him.

5. *The Birth of Jesus* (Lk 2:6-16). The Son of God is born in the poverty of a stable in the town of David, received by the love of the humble Holy Spouses, and adored by poor shepherds.

6. *The Circumcision and Naming of Jesus* (Lk 2:21). The covenant of Abraham and the law are brought to fulfillment with the circumcision of the Son of God on the eighth day. The Holy Spouses give him the name they received from the angel, JESUS, indicating that the fullness of salvation has arrived.

7. *The Presentation of Jesus* (Lk 2:22-35). As the Holy Spouses fulfill all the prescriptions of the Law of the Lord in offering the pure child in the temple, they rejoice at Simeon's prophecy of light for the nations and they grieve at the thought of the sword of rejection.

8. *The Flight to and Return from Egypt* (Mt 2:13-15). The newborn King depends on Joseph to protect him from the bloody earthly king. Returning from Egypt, the Son of God establishes the New Covenant, leading us from the

slavery of sin into the new promised land, his kingdom.

9. *The Finding of Jesus in the Temple* (Lk 2:41-50). At the age of twelve Jesus stays behind in the temple, amazing the teachers by his understanding. His parents, Joseph and Mary, first are anguished at his being lost and then are confronted with the mystery of Jesus' reference to the temple as his "Father's house."

10. *The Hidden Life at Nazareth* (Lk 2:51-52; 3:23). The Incarnate Son of God for thirty years lives obedient to his parents in an ordinary, hidden life of prayer, family, and work, before beginning his public ministry. Mary and Joseph secretly ponder and guard the mystery of God sanctifying our everyday lives[23] and calling us to holiness in the ordinary.

When might this Rosary be prayed?

One suggestion is to use the Holy Spouses Rosary on the days suggested for the joyful mysteries, perhaps mysteries 1-5 on Mondays and mysteries 6-10 on Saturdays.[24] With this suggestion, the luminous, sorrowful, and glorious mysteries of the Marian Rosary would be prayed on the remaining days, as indicated. However, individuals, couples, families, and communities may also pray them whenever most suited to them. This may range from one to ten mysteries daily or weekly. One might also give special attention to the 23rd of each month, since the Feast of the Holy Spouses is celebrated on January 23.[25]

The Mode of Recitation

Pope John Paul II gave beautiful indications for helping make the rosary a fruitful exercise of contemplation.[26] Here we apply these indications to the Holy Spouses Rosary. This prayer guide will make it easy to practice them while praying each mystery.

The Opening

The rosary may begin with the Sign of the Cross, followed by the Apostles' Creed prayed while touching the crucifix. A fundamental article of faith expressed in the Creed is that God's only Son "was conceived of the Holy Spirit, [and] born of the Virgin Mary." This central mystery, shared by the Holy Spouses, is key to all that is contemplated in the mysteries of the Holy Spouses Rosary. On the beads adjacent to the crucifix, a preparatory "Our Father" may follow and then three "Hail Marys" for faith, hope and charity and a "Glory be." These initial prayers, found on page 20, center us on our Catholic faith in the Trinity, the Incarnation, the infused theological virtues, and Mary's motherhood over the Church. This readies us for the individual steps accompanying each mystery.

Announcing Each Mystery

Read the title of the mystery and gaze upon the artistic portrayal of it presented there. Direct your attention and imagination to the physical reality that leads to contact with the mystery of God's presence in human form. Together with Mary and Joseph, share the love and wonder present in that mystery.

Listening to the Word of God

Each of the ten mysteries is totally biblical. Read the Scriptural quotes provided from the infancy narratives of Matthew and Luke. Allow God to speak to you in your particular concrete situation each time you read it.

Silent Reflection

Initially you may read the "Biblical Background" provided, to help understand the Scriptures presented. Also the "Possible Personal Applications" may be helpful for you to identify with the Holy Spouses' role in that mystery, to apply the mystery to yourself, to choose a virtue for which to pray, or persons for whom to pray during that mystery. In any case it is important to have a silent pause of reflection before beginning the vocal prayers for the mystery. Use the "Contemplate" paragraph and the image provided as a mental backdrop for the mystery you are about to pray.

The Our Father

"After listening to the Word and focusing on the mystery, it is natural for the mind to be lifted up toward the Father."[27] Christ and his Holy Family always lead us to the Father. Coming in our midst he makes us his brothers and sisters, able to call God "*Abba*, Father."[28] The "Our Father" joins us with the whole Church in praying the mystery, even when we pray it alone. It is a foundation for our meditation, which unfolds in the tenfold repetition of the Holy Spouses Prayer.

Tenfold Repetition of the Holy Spouses Prayer

This is the most substantial element and the one which most makes it a Holy Spouses rosary. As seen above, the prayer begins with biblical titles. Though addressed to Mary and Joseph, it is totally Christ-centered. It consists of two parts, the first being prayer of praise and the second being prayer of intercessory petition. The center of gravity and the hinge joining these two parts is the name of Jesus. "[I]t is precisely the emphasis given to the name of Jesus and to His mystery that is the sign of a meaningful and fruitful recitation of the Rosary."[29] The Holy Spouses lead us to profess our faith in the God-given name that Joseph bestowed on the child at his circumcision. It is the only name by which we may hope for salvation.[30]

Pope Paul VI encouraged adding to the name of Jesus a phrase referring to the mystery being contemplated.[31] At each mystery we will include an optional biblical or doctrinal title to add to each Holy Spouses prayer for that mystery. In time one may want to substitute one's own phrase instead. The phrases suggested here to correspond to the ten mysteries are: 1) Jesus, the Promised One; 2) Jesus Incarnate; 3) Jesus, the Messiah; 4) Jesus, Son of Man; 5) Jesus, Emmanuel; 6) Jesus, Savior; 7) Jesus, Light of the nations; 8) Jesus, our King; 9) Jesus, Son of God; 10) Jesus, obedient unto death. Such additions may help one to concentrate on each mystery being prayed.

The Glory be

Adoration of the Trinity "is the goal of all Christian contemplation. For Christ is the way that leads us to the Father in the Spirit."[32] This is the summit of contemplation, the purpose for which we were created, and the joy of the Holy Spouses in heaven. The *Glory be* at the end of each mystery could be given its proper prominence by being sung. Notes for a simple plain-chant melody are included.

The Concluding Marellian Invocation

A concluding invocation can help draw spiritual fruits from the contemplation of each mystery. St. Joseph Marello (1844-1895) is the founder of the Oblates of St. Joseph, who present this Holy Spouses Rosary. He introduced the Feast of the Betrothal of the Holy Spouses to the Oblates. He sanctified himself by studying and imitating the humble and hidden virtues of St. Joseph in "serving the interests of Jesus." He preached: "Look at Jesus, Mary, and Joseph, the three greatest persons to live on this earth. What did they do at Nazareth? Nothing that appeared great or extraordinary. They simply performed the humble, ordinary tasks of a poor working family. Yet all their actions were motivated by a spirit of prayerful union with God and therefore took on tremendous glory and worth in the sight of heaven. Hence, it is not a question of doing great and extraordinary things, but of doing God's will in everything. Whether the tasks entrusted to us be great or small, we only need to fulfill God's will in obedience and they will bring us great merit."[33] The most basic purpose of the Holy Spouses Rosary is to help us become saints, inspired by their example and aided by their intercession. For each mystery there will be included a brief concluding invocation for the spiritual fruits indicated by that mystery: "*St. Joseph Marello,* pray for us." This will help us live what we pray.

The Final Prayers

After the mysteries of the Holy Spouses Rosary, one may add the "Hail, Holy Queen" to Mary who represents humanity's highest participation in the salvation Christ won for us. She is honored by the whole heavenly court, beginning with Joseph, her holy spouse. To this may be added the accompanying prayer of Pope Leo XIII, "To you, O Blessed Joseph." There follows the Holy Spouses Litany, and the final prayer, which is adapted from combining the Collect from the Mass of the Holy Spouses and the traditional oration for the Marian Rosary. These prayers are found on page 101, after the individual mysteries.

Importance for Couples and Families Today

This devotion is meant for every individual, and especially for anyone who already is familiar with praying the joyful mysteries of the Marian rosary. It has additional value, however, for families and family prayer. It is uniquely suited to couples, married, engaged, or courting.

Since every Christian community is called to be a genuine school of prayer,[34] it is clear that the most basic of Christian communities, the family, is called to be the first school of prayer. In times when this primary cell of society is under such attack and even threatened by arrogant attempts at unnatural redefinition, contemplation of the Holy Family calls us back to firm grounding in God's beautiful plan for humanity. What Blessed John Paul II wrote about the Marian Rosary is even more pertinent to the Holy Spouses Rosary. It is "a prayer of and for the family."[35] As Fr. Patrick Peyton insisted while promoting the rosary, "the family that prays together stays together." When parents and children together identify with Jesus, Mary, and Joseph, they are better able to grow together in unity, virtue, and covenant love. The image of Jesus Incarnate, subject to human parents, transcends ephemeral video images which often dominate the attention of children and family members. Every family is called to become a holy family with Jesus at the center. The growth and development of the children is entrusted to the intercession of Mary and Joseph, the best of parents and the model for all parents. Broken homes and single-parent families are also assisted by these most excellent spiritual parents. When families passing through strains or crises join in this intercessory prayer, they will find light, strength, and grace to grow beyond their imagining.

The family in God's plan begins with a married couple, joined by God for life in covenant love. The most basic cause of family disintegration is the attack on marriage's inseparable twofold purpose of life and love.[36] Mary and Joseph call couples to center their relationship on Christ. All selfishness, rivalry, and lust must yield to faithful, lifelong commitment in love. In the light of the coming of the Son of God to Mary's womb, children are to be valued as God's great gift. Spouses are called to be generous in receiving children as the greatest fruit and as the crown of their married love.

This rosary may help courting couples remain chaste in their relationship and thereby free to discern God's will with respect to that relationship. They will see marriage as a response to a God-given vocation, rather than simply the satisfaction of one's own desire, which would soon lead to disillusionment. By meditating together on the Holy Spouses Rosary, engaged couples may prepare themselves for a sacramental union built upon faithful commitment and openness to children. Married couples who struggle in their relationship may find healing through this mutual prayer. Whatever the situation, couples who pray the Holy Spouses Rosary have powerful help for growing in virtue.[37]

Opening Prayers and Use of Beads

10 Holy Spouses

Glory Be
St. Marello

Mystery 3 or 8
Our Father

Glory Be
St. Marello

Mystery 4 or 9
Our Father

10 Holy Spouses

10 Holy Spouses

Glory Be
St. Marello

Mystery 2 or 7
Our Father

Mystery 5 or 10
Our Father

Glory Be
St. Marello

10 Holy Spouses

Glory Be
St. Marello

10 Holy Spouses

Concluding Prayers

Glory Be
St. Marello

Mystery 1 or 6
Our Father

3 Hail Marys

Our Father

Sign of the Cross
Apostles' Creed

When recited together with another or others, one person may lead with the italicized parts and the others respond with the parts in normal type.

The Sign of the Cross

While using one's right hand to sign one's body with the cross, forehead, stomach, left shoulder, right shoulder:

> *In the name of the Father, and of the Son, and of the Holy Spirit.* Amen.

On the Cross of the Rosary Beads

> *I believe in God, the Father almighty, Creator of heaven and earth, and in Jesus Christ, his only Son, our Lord,* [bow] *who was conceived by the Holy Spirit, born of the Virgin Mary, suffered under Pontius Pilate, was crucified, died and was buried; he descended into hell; on the third day he rose again from the dead; he ascended into heaven, and is seated at the right hand of God the Father almighty; from there he will come to judge the living and dead.*
>
> I believe in the Holy Spirit, the holy catholic Church, the communion of saints, the forgiveness of sins, the resurrection of the body, and life everlasting. Amen.

On the Bead next to the Cross

Our Father, who art in heaven, hallowed be thy name; thy kingdom come; thy will be done on earth as it is in heaven.

Give us this day our daily bread, and forgive us our trespasses, as we forgive those who trespass against us; and lead us not into temptation, but deliver us from evil. Amen.

On Each of the Three Following Beads

For faith, hope, and charity:

Hail, Mary, full of grace, the Lord is with thee. Blessed art thou among women and blessed is the fruit of thy womb, Jesus.

Holy Mary, Mother of God, pray for us sinners, now and at the hour of our death. Amen.

Between the Three Beads and the Following Bead

Glo-ry be to the Father, and to the Son, and to the Ho-ly Spir-it: as it was

in the be-ginning, is now, and e-ver shall be, world without end. Amen.

Invocation to St. Joseph Marello

> *St. Joseph Marello,*
> pray for us.

Proceed to the announcement and prayer of the individual mysteries, as found on the following pages. End with the concluding prayers, found on page 101.

S·IOSEPH · VIRGO·MARIA·

·IOACHIN· ·S·A

THE FIRST MYSTERY OF THE INCARNATION AND HIDDEN LIFE

The Betrothal

Before the Incarnation the immaculate virgin and the just man are wedded to each other in true married love. The mystery of the Savior's coming into the world begins with a betrothed couple whose relationship is based upon a desire to give themselves entirely to God's love. Without their knowing it, this betrothal was part of the very plan of God.

Listen to the Word of God

*In the sixth month the angel Gabriel was sent from God to a city of Galilee named Nazareth, to a virgin **betrothed** to a man whose name was Joseph, of the house of David; and the virgin's name was Mary (Lk 1:26-27).*

> *Now the birth of Jesus Christ took place
> in this way. When his mother Mary had
> been **betrothed** to Joseph, before they came
> together... (Mt 1:18a).*
>
> *And Joseph also went up from Galilee,
> from the city of Nazareth, to Judea, to the
> city of David, which is called Bethlehem,
> because he was of the house and lineage
> of David, to be enrolled with Mary, his **be-
> trothed**... (Lk 2:4-5a).*

The Biblical Background[38]

Betrothal was the first of two stages for celebrating Jewish marriage in biblical times. It
would take place rather privately in the presence
of immediate family and witnesses. It would involve a formal commitment similar to that of
our wedding vows, but the couple would not immediately cohabit or have conjugal relations. Instead there would be a period of up to a year in
which the groom would prepare a house for his
betrothed, before the second stage of taking her
into his home. During the period of betrothal,
however, the couple could already be referred to
as "husband" and "wife" and they enjoyed all the
same legal benefits.

Matthew and Luke are the only two Gospel
writers who deal with the infancy of Jesus. Each

of them considers it important to report that Mary and Joseph are betrothed and that Joseph is of the line of David. The promised Messiah or Christ had to come from the house of David, according to the prophecy made to David through the prophet Nathan, that God would raise up offspring after him and establish the throne of his kingdom forever.[39] Lineage was always traced through the father. Even in irregular cases, marriage to a child's mother established fatherhood. The two facts of Joseph's davidic descent and of his betrothal to Mary are the guarantors that any offspring of Mary can rightly claim to be a "son of David."

Possible Personal Applications

At the time of their betrothal, Mary and Joseph did not know what God had in store for them, but the immaculate virgin and the just man shared a common faith in God and a common desire to give themselves entirely to God through their gift of self to each other.

This mystery calls us to appreciate God's plan for love and life. Marriage is a vocation that should be approached in chastity. It is not self-serving, but self-giving. Engaged couples are to center their relationship on the will of God. His promise is often fulfilled in ways we never expect or even imagine. When we center our lives in his will, we too may be instruments for Christ to become present in our world.

During this mystery we may pray for chastity for all individuals and particularly for couples entering into a relationship or already engaged. We pray that couples and each of us may seek God's will always and in everything.

Dear Mary and Joseph, help us to understand better our call and to respond chastely to our vocation, trusting fully in God's will for us.

Contemplate

Imagine Mary's gratitude and her trust that her love for Joseph would express and support her most pure love for God. Think how Joseph must have considered himself the most blessed man in the world to be betrothed to most holy Mary. Admire their unconditional commitment to each other according to God's plan. Meditate with the Holy Spouses on the wonder of God's call for you and the promise of unforeseen blessings still to come to you through your faithfulness to your vocation.

The *Our Father*

Meditative Tenfold Repetition of the *Holy Spouses Prayer*

Mary, full of grace, and Joseph, son of David; honor to you, Mother of God, and to you, guardian of the Redeemer. Eternal praise to the child with whom you formed a family, JESUS, THE PROMISED ONE.

Holy Spouses, pray for us sinners, our families and communities, now and at the hour of our death. Amen.

The Glory Be

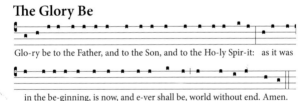

Glo-ry be to the Father, and to the Son, and to the Ho-ly Spir-it: as it was

in the be-ginning, is now, and e-ver shall be, world without end. Amen.

Invocation to St. Joseph Marello

St. Joseph Marello,
pray for us.

THE SECOND MYSTERY OF THE INCARNATION AND HIDDEN LIFE

The Annunciation to Mary

God chooses the virgin Mary, betrothed to Joseph of the house of David, for the miracle of his coming in human flesh. The Son of God becomes dependant on acceptance by a human mother, and thereupon takes the nature of a tiny being in her womb.

Listen to the Word of God

[The angel Gabriel came to Mary] and said, "Hail, full of grace, the Lord is with you!" But she was greatly troubled at the saying, and considered in her mind what sort of greeting this might be. And the angel said to her, "Do not fear, Mary, for you have found favor with God. And behold, you will conceive in your womb and bear a son, and you shall call his name Jesus. He will be great, and will be called the Son of

*the Most High; and the Lord God will give
to him the throne of his father David, and
he will reign over the house of Jacob for
ever; and of his kingdom there will be no
end." And Mary said to the angel, "How
shall this be, since I have no carnal knowl-
edge of my betrothed?" And the angel said
to her, "The Holy Spirit will come upon
you, and the power of the Most High will
overshadow you; therefore the child to be
born will be called holy, the Son of God.
And behold, your kinswoman Elizabeth in
her old age has also conceived a son; and
this is the sixth month with her who was
called barren. For with God nothing will
be impossible." And Mary said, "Behold, I
am the handmaid of the Lord; let it be to
me according to your word"* (Lk 1:28-38).

The Biblical Background

God's messenger greets Mary with the astound-
ing words that she is "full of grace," or fully favored
by God, words that she could not totally fathom,
and words that we understand in light of the de-
veloped doctrine of the Immaculate Conception.[40]
As is usual with announcements of birth and vocation in the Bible, these first words of the angel indicate her most important quality with respect to the

mission to be entrusted to her. Her freedom from stain of sin most fittingly equips her to be mother to the all-holy Son of God. Also standard are the words "Do not fear." Mary is to trust God in her mission of conceiving in her womb and bearing Jesus, the awaited davidic king. Mary would naturally presume that davidic lineage would be passed through Joseph, her betrothed.

Yet, Mary searches for more clarity about what she is to do. How is the conception to come about? The words "I do not know man" are the common biblical expression for stating that she has not had relations with her betrothed. She remains a "virgin," as Luke has already taken care to state. It is at this point that the angel communicates the most overwhelming news of all: the child is the very Son of God, and is to be conceived virginally by the Holy Spirit! As a sign that all is possible for God, Mary is told that her elderly, barren relative, Elizabeth, has already conceived.

In faith, Mary bows humbly and obediently before the power of the Most High and accepts his Son into her womb.

Possible Personal Applications

Mary has no opportunity for consultation with Joseph, before accepting God's Son into her womb.

She knows her betrothed as a man of faith, and trusts him enough to presume that he will accept her and the child and raise Jesus together with her. Mary's extraordinary encounter with God's unfathomable plan deepens her faith. This challenge to their plans for their marriage also deepens her love and trust in her betrothed. St. Marello states that, without knowing it, Joseph too was given special graces at the time of the annunciation to Mary.[41]

Mary teaches all of us the importance of remaining in the state of grace and of following our vocation wherever it leads. She teaches us to listen to the Lord in prayer and to accept whatever challenges are presented. May we too say a humble "yes" to the Lord as his humble servants.

In this mystery we may pray for all young ladies to make wise and God-centered choices with regard to their vocation, reverencing virginity and the sacredness of marriage and child-bearing. We may pray for all wives and mothers, and for all women called to celibacy. We all pray for a more humble and complete collaboration with God's plan for us.

Dear Mary and Joseph, pray that we may more closely imitate you in the virtue of obedience, always listening to God's will and following it in faith.

Contemplate

Reflect upon Mary's humble heart filled with wonder at the appearance of the angel Gabriel choosing her for the greatest of all human missions. Admire the unreserved availability expressed in her *fiat*, "let it be done to me." With Mary exult in the greatness of God's love poured out for you through his Son come to be in her womb.

The *Our Father*

Meditative Tenfold Repetition of the *Holy Spouses Prayer*

Mary, full of grace, and Joseph, son of David; honor to you, Mother of God, and to you, guardian of the Redeemer. Eternal praise to the child with whom you formed a family, JESUS, INCARNATE.

Holy Spouses, pray for us sinners, our families and communities, now and at the hour of our death. Amen.

The Glory Be

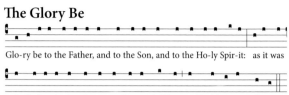

Glo-ry be to the Father, and to the Son, and to the Ho-ly Spir-it: as it was

in the be-ginning, is now, and e-ver shall be, world without end. Amen.

Invocation to St. Joseph Marello

St. Joseph Marello,
pray for us.

THE THIRD MYSTERY OF THE INCARNATION AND HIDDEN LIFE

The Annunciation to Joseph

God's design is for Mary's husband, the just man of the house of David, to continue with their plans to form a home together, and to name and act as father to the child conceived by the Holy Spirit.

Listen to the Word of God

…she was found to be with child of the Holy Spirit; and her husband Joseph, being a just man and unwilling to shame her, resolved to release her quietly. But as he considered this, behold, an angel of the Lord appeared to him in a dream, saying, "Joseph, son of David, do not fear to take Mary your wife even though that which is conceived in her is indeed of the Holy Spirit. She will bear a son, whom you will give the name Jesus, for he will save his people from their sins." All this took place to fulfil

what the Lord had spoken by the prophet:
"Behold, a virgin shall conceive and bear
a son, and his name shall be called "Em-
manuel" (which means, "God with us")
(Mt 1:18b-23).

The Biblical Background

Most current translations facilitate the common interpretation that Joseph saw Mary pregnant, suspected her of infidelity, and decided to divorce her. This "suspicion interpretation" presumes that Mary would not have told him about the appearance of the angel to her.

However, after the profound experience of the annunciation that would so deeply affect not only her but also her betrothed, she would most likely feel obliged in justice to reveal this mystery to him, if to no one else. Based only on her faith in the angel's message, even before any physical signs of pregnancy, Mary would trustingly share this overwhelming experience with her beloved betrothed. The angel had mentioned that her child would be given "the throne of his father David," indirectly indicating that Joseph of the house of David would be a part of this mystery. Their married love was based upon their shared faith and openness to God. Joseph then did not receive two separate pieces of information, first that Mary was pregnant and only later that it was by the Holy Spirit; he was told the single fact that she was "with child of the Holy Spirit." The virginal conception would be a secret shared between husband and wife and revealed to no one, perhaps until after Pentecost when Mary would be able to tell the apostles who by then had received the same Holy Spirit that she had encountered at her annunciation.

Instead of the suspicion interpretation, there is the "reverent awe" interpretation.[42] Translations must decide where to insert punctuation, which does not occur in the original Greek, and must interpret conjunctions which have multiple usages. The above translation is just as faithful to the original text. Joseph is a "just man," which in the Bible means that he was a man of faith, who believed in God's promise and was willing to act upon it in obedience, like Abel, Noah, Abraham, Jacob, Joseph (the patriarch), and David. He decided to release Mary from their betrothal vows, not because he suspected her of unfaithfulness, but because he believed with her that God's Son had been conceived virginally in her womb. This naturally filled him with awe and the recognition of his own unworthiness. Faced with the Incarnation, he could not presume to continue with his plans for the marriage. He could not on his own claim to act as father to the divine child conceived by the Holy Spirit. By no means did he wish to shame Mary or to stand in the way of the Mother of God. As painful as it would be, Joseph was willing to make the great sacrifice of separating from the love of his life, if it were the will of God and for her good.

The angel of God comes to Joseph in a dream, addressing him by the title important to his mission, "son of David." He is to guarantee that the child be of the line of David, able to be recognized as the Christ. Like Mary, he is also told not to fear the vocation being communicated to him. He is to continue with plans for the second stage of the marriage, by taking Mary into his home. He is to name the child, and act as father to the Savior, "God-with-us."

Possible Personal Applications

Young men (and all men) have in Joseph a model who seeks not his own pleasure, but the good of others all according to God's plan. He is a man of faith. He has lived a chaste betrothal. He trusts and loves Mary so much that he is willing to make any sacrifice necessary. He listens to God prayerfully. He is ready to accept the responsibility of husband and father.

Men who are courting or engaged are called like Joseph to respect their girlfriends or fiancées. Joseph models the truly profound respect for women that all men are called to have. This respect sees the immense value of a woman's soul and naturally leads to chastity. Chastity is essential for allowing love to grow and deepen. A loving relationship is rooted in God's will, and never in sin. True love between a man and woman always involves helping each other grow in virtue. Love involves sacrifice and self-giving, rather than self-seeking. All dating should be recognized in the context of a possible call to marriage. This vocation in its essence is a life-long union in love and in openness to receive and to parent children together. Every relationship must meet the test of being in accord with God's plan; if not in accord, it must be discontinued.

In this mystery we may pray for all young men, especially those courting or engaged, to follow the example of Joseph in making godly decisions to live according to these truths.

Joseph's example invites everyone to listen to God in prayer, especially before any major decision. We are all called to be willing to sacrifice our own plans and desires, if they should not be in harmony with God's plan. Each of us must search prayerfully for our mission in the concrete circumstances of our daily lives.

Dear Mary and Joseph, pray that we may culti-vate a greater respect and willingness to sacrifice for others, especially in our closest relationships.

Contemplate

Imagine Joseph with Mary overwhelmed at the long-awaited news of the arrival of the Messiah. Fathom his reverent awe at the angel affirming his mission as husband to the Mother of God and earthly father to the Son of God. Enter with Joseph into gratitude for God's never-ending faithfulness to his promises. Adore the Christ who has come to save you from your sins.

The *Our Father*

Meditative Tenfold Repetition of the *Holy Spouses Prayer*

Mary, full of grace, and Joseph, son of David; honor to you, Mother of God, and to you, guardian of the Redeemer. Eternal praise to the child with whom you formed a family, JESUS, THE MESSIAH.

Holy Spouses, pray for us sinners, our families and communities, now and at the hour of our death. Amen.

The Glory Be

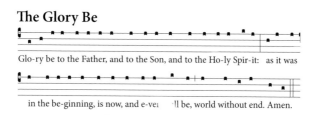

Glo-ry be to the Father, and to the Son, and to the Ho-ly Spir-it: as it was

in the be-ginning, is now, and e-ver ᐧll be, world without end. Amen.

Invocation to St. Joseph Marello

St. Joseph Marello, pray for us.

THE FOURTH MYSTERY OF THE INCARNATION AND HIDDEN LIFE

Joseph Takes Mary his Wife into his Home

The Son of God depends upon a chosen human father, committed in a virginal marriage, to provide a loving, caring, and wholesome home for him.

Listen to the Word of God

When Joseph woke from sleep, he did as the angel of the Lord commanded him; he took his wife, but knew her not until she had borne a son; and he called his name Jesus (Mt 1:24-25).

The Biblical Background

Matthew communicates clearly and succinctly here (and also after Joseph's later dreams) that Joseph obeys the Lord's angel unquestioningly, immediately, and faithfully. We have no words of Joseph recorded, as we do for Mary, but his actions are evidence of his *fiat* similar to her "let it be to me according to your word." Whereas Mary's feminine role is that of receiving the Son of God in her womb, Joseph's masculine role is active, in this case not in the biological sense, but still in the spousal and parental sense of "taking his wife" and naming their child. The words used to describe Joseph's actions repeat exactly the angel's instructions. Joseph does exactly what God calls him to do.

Although Joseph's action is immediate and joyful, it is not without its sacrifice. Even while he "takes his wife" according to the final stage of celebrating marriage, he does not have conjugal relations with her as would be customary for that stage. Rather "he knew her not," thus accepting virginity along with the vocation to be husband and father. (The biblical word "until" does not imply that he had relations with her after Jesus was born.)[43]

The virginity mentioned by both Matthew and Luke does not regard simply the conception of Jesus, but is a condition of their beginning life together as a married couple. Their marriage is to be uniquely virginal, in light of the virginal conception. All the world may presume that they had marital relations and even that Jesus was conceived in the normal way as "Joseph's son," but Mary and Joseph lovingly guard the secret, treasure it, and build their married love upon it. Their virginity in this extraordinary case certainly does not lessen the reality of their marriage. Rather than diminish their married love, it deepens it with their constant awareness of God's eternal love, of which every marriage is to be an earthly sign. In this spousal love, together they parent God's Son, to whom Joseph in faith gave the name of "Jesus," Savior.

Possible Personal Applications

In his prompt, unquestioning obedience, Joseph is a model for all of us. When God's will is clear to us through his commandments, the moral teaching of his Church, the sound advice of a confessor, or a well-discerned personal calling, we are not to hesitate. Trusting that God is all-loving and certainly knows better than we do, we should decide and set out to follow his will fully. This is true for decisions in our everyday lives, but is of paramount importance for vocational decisions about our permanent state of life.

Both marriage and consecrated virginity involve a covenant commitment. Marriage consists of a total, unconditional gift of self to one's spouse until death. It begins with public and sacred vows made in the presence of God and the Church. Only then are husband and wife to begin to live together and celebrate their sacramental unity through sexual intimacy open to life.

While all are called to virginity until validly married, some are called to a permanent vocation of consecrated virginity in the priesthood or religious life. Joseph teaches those who are called to this life to trust in the Lord and not to fear to embrace joyfully this special friendship with him. God's love will not fail to fill, sustain, and gladden those he calls. The state of virginal marriage to Christ and his body the Church is able to encounter love also in the many people one is able to serve or pray for. Priests, Sisters, and Brothers richly experience spiritual parenthood in their lives and ministry.

The virginity of the Holy Spouses also inspires married couples to marital chastity, which involves faithfulness, self-giving, physical intimacy according to moral parameters, and periodic abstinence when indicated.

Joseph and Mary invite couples to be generous in accepting life, even in complicated and special situations. Life is always an incomparable, precious gift. It is never to be made secondary to concerns over material goods or comfort. Every zygote conceived in the womb is a precious image of God, with an immortal soul. The Holy Spouses are the co-patrons of life in the womb. God's plan is for all life to be received, protected and nurtured by a loving father and mother, joined together in lifelong marriage. Even when "mistakes" are made, no human being is ever a mistake, but always deserving of love.

In this mystery we may pray for couples entering into marriage, for those called to special vocations of consecrated virginity, for a renewed acceptance of lifelong commitment, for an appreciation of the Sacraments of Matrimony and Holy Orders and also of the Consecrated Life, for growth in the virtue of chastity, for parents, and for respect for the life of the unborn. In a word, we all pray to better imitate Joseph's prompt, unquestioning obedience to God's call.

Dear Mary and Joseph, help us prepare our hearts and our homes to welcome your Son, Jesus. We ask your intercession to grow in the virtues of chastity and responsiveness to God's call.

Contemplate

Picture young Joseph and Mary coming to live together as pure spouses to provide a family for the Son of God to be born to them. Imagine how God's overwhelming love for them so deepens their love for each other. With the Holy Spouses stand in awe at the mystery of God coming to us as the Son of Man in Mary's womb.

The *Our Father*

Meditative Tenfold Repetition of the *Holy Spouses Prayer*

Mary, full of grace, and Joseph, son of David; honor to you, Mother of God, and to you, guardian of the Redeemer. Eternal praise to the child with whom you formed a family, JESUS, SON OF MAN.

Holy Spouses, pray for us sinners, our families and communities, now and at the hour of our death. Amen.

The Glory Be

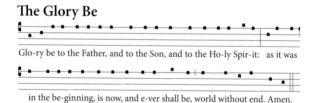

Glo-ry be to the Father, and to the Son, and to the Ho-ly Spir-it: as it was

in the be-ginning, is now, and e-ver shall be, world without end. Amen.

Invocation to St. Joseph Marello

St. Joseph Marello,
pray for us.

THE FIFTH MYSTERY OF THE INCARNATION AND HIDDEN LIFE

The Birth of Jesus

The Son of God is born in the poverty of a stable in the town of David, received by the love of the humble Holy Spouses, and adored by poor shepherds.

Listen to the Word of God

And while [Mary and Joseph] were [in Bethlehem], the time came for her to be delivered. And she gave birth to her first-born son and wrapped him in swaddling cloths, and laid him in a manger, because there was no place for them in the inn. And in that region there were shepherds out in the field, keeping watch over their flock by night. And an angel of the Lord appeared to them, and the glory of the Lord shone around them, and they were filled with fear. And the angel said to them, "Be not afraid; for behold, I bring you good

*news of a great joy which will come to all
the people; for to you is born this day in
the city of David a Savior, who is Christ
the Lord. And this will be a sign for you:
you will find a babe wrapped in swaddling
cloths and lying in a manger." And sud-
denly there was with the angel a multitude
of the heavenly host praising God and
saying, "Glory to God in the highest, and
on earth peace among men with whom he
is pleased!" When the angels went away
from them into heaven, the shepherds said
to one another, "Let us go over to Bethlehem and see this thing that has happened,
which the Lord has made known to us."
And they went with haste, and found Mary
and Joseph, and the babe lying in a manger* (Lk 2:6-16).

The Biblical Background

Bethlehem is the city of David (1 Sam 17:12). The
promise of the coming of the Messiah in David's
line is fittingly fulfilled not only by his legal descent
from Joseph of the house of David, but also by his
actual birth in that city (cf. also Mt 2:5-6). The oc-
casion is a census for which Joseph and his family
must report to his ancestral town. Jesus is registered
as a member of the human race, which he is born
to save.[44]

However, there is no room for him in the *katáluma*, a word usually translated "inn" here, whereas for the Last Supper the same word is translated "upper room" (Lk 22:11-12, Mk 14:14). Perhaps there is no room on the upper level where people lodge, so that his birth must take place below at ground level where the animals are kept. Mary and Joseph lay the newborn Jesus in a manger, which is a feeding trough for animals, perhaps already symbolic of the fact that he has come to be our Bread of Life (Jn 6:35).

Rejection in the inn at Jesus' birth in this world is a prelude to the ultimate rejection of the cross at the end of his earthly life. The material poverty of the setting indicates God's love identifying with us in our struggles. The only ones to receive a heavenly invitation to the transcendental event are poor shepherds. Untold divine wealth and glory totally overshadow the meager surroundings. Mary and Joseph's own experience of angelic messages is confirmed by that of the shepherds. In the most humble of circumstances there is the great joy of the birth of the Savior for all people. For the first time "Mary and Joseph and the babe" are visible as the Holy Family, a sign of glory and great joy. The Holy Spouses receive Christ the Lord to treasure and they secretly share with each other the mystery of God's love Incarnate.

Possible Personal Applications

Despite the situation of oppressive laws imposed by a foreign power, Joseph and Mary obey the civil authorities. They teach us to be respectful citizens and to contribute our part toward public order and the common good.

Entrusted with the role of provider and protector, Joseph does everything in his power to provide a worthy place for the imminent birth, but ultimately he relies humbly and trustingly on God to determine how and where this child will be born. If we struggle with poverty or difficult situations or rejection, the Holy Spouses teach us to accept humiliations, to persevere with trust in Divine Providence, and to appreciate the priceless blessings that often accompany dire circumstances.

The birth of the Son of God Incarnate evidences God's love for every human being in the womb. Christ identifies with every child conceived. Every child must be allowed to be born; no matter what the circumstances be, direct abortion can never be justified.

Husbands and wives are called to be open to collaborate with God in receiving new human life to love and nurture. Children are the crown and the greatest fruit of marriage. Every child is to be treasured as a brother or sister of Jesus, who also became a little child. All parents are to love their children after the example of Mary and Joseph's love for Jesus.

As Mary, Joseph, and the shepherds adored Jesus, the Bread of Life lying in the manger, so are we able to adore the same Jesus given us in the Holy Eucharist. St. Marello invites us to receive Jesus in Holy Communion with the same love with which St. Joseph held him so tenderly in his arms.[45] As the shepherds traveled to visit the babe and see the marvels there, so may we make visits to Jesus in the Blessed Sacrament in the tabernacles of our churches. Every holy hour is a sharing in the good news of great joy: our Savior is there for us!

In this mystery we may pray for parents to receive their babies with love, for parents who have been wounded by the terrible error of abortion, for spouses to be open to children and raise them with devotion, for infertile couples to trust in God's plan for life-giving in their relationship, for a spirit of poverty that treasures eternal wealth, and for reverent awareness of the Real Presence of Jesus in the Blessed Sacrament.

Dear Mary and Joseph, help us to adore the Bread of Life, to treasure all human life, and to face difficulties with humility, patience, and trust.

Contemplate

With the Holy Spouses witness how the poverty of the Nativity only serves the more to appreciate God's infinite love poured out for us through the birth of his Son. With Mary, Joseph, and the shepherds experience the great joy of Emmanuel,

God-with-us. With them adore your Savior, Christ the Lord.

The *Our Father*

Meditative Tenfold Repetition of the *Holy Spouses Prayer*

Mary, full of grace, and Joseph, son of David; honor to you, Mother of God, and to you, guardian of the Redeemer. Eternal praise to the child with whom you formed a family, JESUS, EMMANUEL.

Holy Spouses, pray for us sinners, our families and communities, now and at the hour of our death. Amen.

The Glory Be

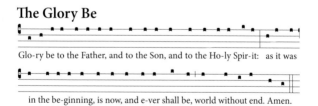

Glo-ry be to the Father, and to the Son, and to the Ho-ly Spir-it: as it was

in the be-ginning, is now, and e-ver shall be, world without end. Amen.

Invocation to St. Joseph Marello

St. Joseph Marello,
pray for us.

The Circumcision and Naming of Jesus

> *The covenant of Abraham and the law are brought to fulfillment with the circumcision of the Son of God on the eighth day. The Holy Spouses give him the name they received from the angel, JESUS, indicating that the fullness of salvation has arrived.*

Listen to the Word of God

> *And when the eight days for his circumcision were accomplished, he was called Jesus, the name given by the angel before he was conceived in the womb* (Lk 2:21).

The Biblical Background[46]

From the time of God's covenant with Abraham, it was first of all the father's duty to circumcise his son as a sign of that covenant (Gn 17:10-13).

Clearly underlying Luke's single verse regarding Jesus' circumcision is Leviticus 12:3, prescribing that for every newborn male child "on the eighth day the flesh of his foreskin shall be circumcised." Luke presents the verse, however, in parallel to a much longer passage regarding the circumcision of John the Baptist (Lk 1:59-79). Whereas Luke uses the exact time marker from Leviticus to state that John was circumcised "on the eighth day" (1:59), in the case of Jesus he changes the wording to the more symbolic language of fulfillment, "when the eight days ... were *accomplished*." This language hints that not only the eight days are complete, but that the circumcision of this child also brings to completion the law and covenant originally sealed with Abraham. The verse does not even state directly that Jesus was circumcised, but uses impersonal language to avoid Jesus being introduced into the covenant by others. *He* is the one who has come to establish the new covenant that awaited fulfillment since Abraham and that was announced by the prophets.[47] The blood shed at the circumcision also prefigured the cross and also our initiation into the new covenant through Baptism.[48]

The circumcision of Jesus is mentioned in a clause grammatically subordinate to the main verb "he was called." The circumcision and naming are two complementary aspects of the mystery of salvation. The meaning and origin of the name "Jesus" help illustrate and explain the fulfillment indicated by the circumcision. Biblical names indicate a person's identity and mission. At the annunciation in Luke Mary is told to name the child "Jesus," but the name is never applied to him before the circumcision. In Matthew's Gospel, Joseph is given the reason and meaning of the name: "you shall call his name Jesus, for he will save his people from their sins" (1:21). In this child is the mystery of God come in our midst to bring us the salvation that only God can give. Luke breaks his literary parallels by not saying that Mary named him as she was told. He uses instead the passive "he was called Jesus" without indicating who did the naming. This calls us to go beyond the human agents and realize that it is "the name given by the angel before he was conceived in the womb."

From Matthew we know that Joseph did the actual naming: "he called his name 'Jesus'" (1:25). In this he acted on behalf of God the Father, the angel, Mary, and himself, applying the name chosen from all eternity.

Possible Personal Applications

Often people do not consider St. Joseph as Jesus' "real" father, since he did not physically engender him. Joseph, more than anyone else, was aware that this son did not come from him, but from God. This child was the fulfillment of all that had been promised, and Joseph was totally aware that he was unworthy to act as the child's father. He also knew, however, that God was calling him to this ministry. In humble, obedient, and loving service, he accepted Mary his wife and the child. Through the rite of circumcision and the act of naming Jesus, Joseph was fulfilling his role as father and accepting all the responsibilities that accompanied that role.

We must ask the intercession of the Holy Spouses in our times, when many men are engendering children through illicit sexual relations, seeking pleasure without responsibility. Some never even know that they have conceived a child. This terrible injustice cries to heaven for vengeance, for God to "turn the hearts of fathers back to their children" (Mal 4:6, or 3:24 in the Septuagint).

There is no greater counter-example to this selfishness than St. Joseph, the holy spouse. His acceptance of the child conceived and born within their marriage teaches us that in God's plan children deserve to have a father and mother who are married and who will love one another for the rest of their lives.

In giving Jesus the name willed by God, Joseph and Mary teach parents their duty together to give a name to their child, as God wills. While conception outside marriage is a mistake, no child is ever to be considered a "mistake." Every human conceived is in the image of God, of precious worth in his sight. As Jesus was known as "son of Joseph," so too every child deserves to be known as a child of loving parents. Jesus says: "whoever receives one such child in my name receives me" (Mt 18:5). He also gives his harshest warning for anyone who harms a child: "it would be better for him to have a great millstone tied around his neck and to be drowned in the depth of the sea" (Mt 18:6; Lk 17:2). The Holy Spouses teach parents to "do the right thing": to listen to God, to trust his will and to follow it with commitment all throughout life.

Among the first and greatest honors and responsibilities of parents is that of baptizing their babies as soon as possible after birth. The Rite of Baptism begins with parents stating together the name they give their child before God and the Church.

For those children whose biological fathers have failed them, Joseph may inspire other men to honorably marry their mothers and act as "real" fathers to the children they have not engendered. Children who remain without any father may seek consolation and strength in looking to St. Joseph as their spiritual father, while those without a loving mother may turn to Mary.

Dear Mary and Joseph, pray for us that we may always reverence the Name of Jesus, fulfill our responsibilities, and live our baptismal commitment as members of his Body.

Contemplate

Share the Holy Spouses' awe at the child who has come to fulfill the law and the covenant that for two millennia was signified by circumcision. Experience their wonder as the painful shedding of a drop of his blood already signifies the salvation indicated by the very Name that God chose for him. With Mary and Joseph adore Jesus your Savior.

The *Our Father*

Meditative Tenfold Repetition of the *Holy Spouses Prayer*

Mary, full of grace, and Joseph, son of David; honor to you, Mother of God, and to you, guardian of the Redeemer. Eternal praise to the child with whom you formed a family, JESUS, SAVIOR.

Holy Spouses, pray for us sinners, our families and communities, now and at the hour of our death. Amen.

The Glory Be

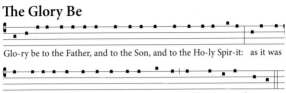

Glo-ry be to the Father, and to the Son, and to the Ho-ly Spir-it: as it was

in the be-ginning, is now, and e-ver shall be, world without end. Amen.

Invocation to St. Joseph Marello

St. Joseph Marello,
pray for us.

THE SEVENTH MYSTERY OF THE INCARNATION AND HIDDEN LIFE

The Presentation of Jesus

As the Holy Spouses fulfill all the prescriptions of the Law of the Lord in offering the pure child in the temple, they rejoice at Simeon's prophecy of light for the nations and they grieve at the thought of the sword of re, ˉtion.

Listen to the Word of God

And when the days were accomplished for their purification according to the law of Moses, they brought him up to Jerusalem to present him to the Lord (as it is written in the law of the Lord, "Every male that opens the womb shall be called holy to the Lord") and to offer a sacrifice according to what is said in the law of the Lord, "a pair of turtledoves, or two young pigeons." Now there was a man in Jerusalem, whose name was Simeon, and this

*man was righteous and devout, looking
for the consolation of Israel, and the Holy
Spirit was upon him. And it had been
revealed to him by the Holy Spirit that he
should not see death before he had seen the
Lord's Christ. And inspired by the Spirit
he came into the temple; and when the
parents brought in the child Jesus, to do for
him according to the custom of the law, he
took him up in his arms and blessed God
and said, "Lord, now let your servant de-
part in peace, according to your word; for
mine eyes have seen your salvation which
you have prepared in the presence of all
peoples, a light for revelation to the Gen-
tiles, and for glory to your people Israel."
And his father and his mother marveled
at what was said about him; and Simeon
blessed them and said to Mary his mother,
"Behold, this child is set for the fall and rising of many in Israel, and for a sign that
is spoken against (and a sword will pierce
through your own soul also), that thoughts
out of many hearts may be revealed"* (Lk
2:22-35).

The Biblical Background

As in the previous verse for the circumcision,
this passage too begins with fulfillment language.

Not only the time for purification is completed, but Old Testament prophecy, Mosaic Law, and priestly worship are all completed with Jesus being offered in the Temple. The book of Malachi prophesied that the day of the Lord would come to purify the insincere worship of the priests and correct the sins of the people who divorced their Israelite wives to marry pagans. The child Jesus himself is the "pure offering" (Mal 1:11) come to the temple. He replaces the flawed and incomplete offering of animals.

The setting as described by Luke uses impersonal language that mixes together the law for the purification of the mother on the fortieth day after giving birth (Lev 12:1ff) and the law for the presentation or consecration of the firstborn male (Ex 13:1,11ff), who could also be bought back (Ex 13:15; Num 18:15-16). The subject of the first sentence is "they," referring to Joseph and Mary, so that the uncommon reference to "their purification" simply indicates that both Joseph and Mary participate together in fulfilling all the prescriptions "according to the law of Moses," which was "the law of the Lord," as Luke will repeat several times. As obedient Jews, they present Jesus to the Lord, offering the sacrifice of two turtledoves in his stead. This offering already symbolizes his final offering of himself on the cross in our stead, to buy us back for God.

Holy Simeon recognizes Jesus as the Savior, revealing light and glory for the nations. Mary and Joseph marvel and receive his blessing, but also hear of the judgment and the sword of sorrow that will pierce Mary's heart, a warning that will be fulfilled as Mary stands at the foot of Jesus' cross after Joseph has already passed from this earth.

Possible Personal Applications

With Mary and Joseph we see the unfolding of the mystery of God's love in this little child. He is the purest offering come from God. He belongs to God, and they unreservedly present him back to God. They do everything possible to follow the will of God in his regard. Having claimed no exemption from civil law with respect to the census, they certainly claim no exemption from any of the religious laws they hold in esteem. As poor, obedient, and loving parents, they travel to the holy city to offer two birds to buy him back from the temple.

Through their faith and obedience the Holy Spouses encounter another divine manifestation, subsequent to their revelations first from the angel and then from the shepherds. Simeon and Anna, moved by the Holy Spirit, witness to the divinity of their child and his saving mission to the entire world. Mary and Joseph "marveled at what was said about him," and with them we too marvel at this mystery of the light of the world hidden in the form of a small baby. How privileged we are that his glory and salvation are revealed to us through faith!

By our obedience to the will of God, expressed in divine law and church precepts and our own vocation, we too offer ourselves to the Lord. Infinitely surpassing temple worship, our participation in the Eucharist allows us to offer the pure sacrifice of Jesus to the Father. Through this offering we are redeemed or bought back from the slavery to sin and death.

In this mystery we may pray for an increase of generosity and self-sacrifice. We pray for parents to realize that their children belong to God, to present their children to the Lord for Baptism during the first days after birth, and to teach their children by word and example to practice the faith, obeying the commandments and the precepts of the Church.

Dear Mary and Joseph, help us to offer ourselves to the Lord, to place our loved ones in his hands, and to do our part to support parenthood, religious upbringing of children, and family life.

Contemplate

Marvel with the Holy Spouses at the Light of the Nations come to us as a small baby. Consider how at the presentation of the gifts of bread and wine at every Eucharist we are to unite the offering of ourselves to Christ's self-oblation to the Father.

The *Our Father*

Meditative Tenfold Repetition of the *Holy Spouses Prayer*

Mary, full of grace, and Joseph, son of David; honor to you, Mother of God, and to you, guardian of the Redeemer. Eternal praise to the child with whom you formed a family, JESUS, LIGHT OF THE NATIONS.

Holy Spouses, pray for us sinners, our families and communities, now and at the hour of our death. Amen.

The Glory Be

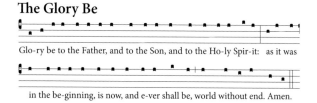

Glo-ry be to the Father, and to the Son, and to the Ho-ly Spir-it: as it was

in the be-ginning, is now, and e-ver shall be, world without end. Amen.

Invocation to St. Joseph Marello

St. Joseph Marello,
pray for us.

THE EIGHTH MYSTERY OF THE INCARNATION AND HIDDEN LIFE

The Flight to and Return from Egypt

> *The newborn King depends on Joseph to protect him from the bloody earthly king. Returning from Egypt, the Son of God establishes the New Covenant, leading us from the slavery of sin into the new promised land, his kingdom.*

Listen to the Word of God

Now when [the wise men] had departed, behold, an angel of the Lord appeared to Joseph in a dream and said, "Rise, take the child and his mother, and flee to Egypt, and remain there till I tell you; for Herod is about to search for the child, to destroy him." And he rose and took the child and his mother by night, and departed to Egypt, and remained there until the death of Herod. This was to fulfil what the Lord had spoken by the prophet, "Out of Egypt have I called my son" (Mt 2:13-15).

The Biblical Background[49]

After Jesus' birth, bloody King Herod's murderous jealousy of "the newborn king of the Jews" is met by the angel of the Lord again speaking to Joseph in a dream. The angel's instructions are to flee into Egypt, which historically is a place of idolatry, but also a place of refuge from famine and from murderous kings.[50] As commanded and necessary, Joseph again obeyed immediately, setting out for Egypt without any time for planning or preparation.

As with everything associated with the Redeemer of the world, there was a cosmic and transcendent level present in the midst of this human history of fleeing for one's life and struggling to survive in a foreign land. The Gospel explains that "This was to fulfill what the Lord had spoken by the prophet, 'Out of Egypt have I called my son.'" The quote is from Hosea, a prophetic book which begins with the image of an unfaithful wife, representing the people Israel, whom God in his love nevertheless promises to take back. The particular verse quoted is from Hosea 11:1, referring to Israel as God's son, lovingly called forth from Egypt during the time of Moses and the Exodus (see also Ex 4:22). The passage describes Israel's unfaithfulness in "burning incense to idols" and in seeking protection by allying with Egypt instead of trusting in the Lord. God's just anger is again tempered by his loving promise "Out of Egypt they shall come trembling … and I will resettle them in their homes" (Hos 11:11).

While the immediate purpose of going to Egypt was to save Jesus from death at the hands of Herod, the providential purpose was to show the fulfillment of God's loving plan. Herod died and the angel of the Lord advised Joseph to return to the land of Israel. As God's son, Israel, had sought refuge in Egypt and come forth from Egypt to enter into his covenant love, so now God's Son, Jesus, came out of refuge in Egypt to establish "a new covenant" that made the first covenant obsolete.[51] The flight to and the return from Egypt show from the start that the Savior had come for all the peoples of the world. God's Son, who had come to "save his people from their sins," entered the center of idolatry, taking the identity of Israel upon himself so as to redeem it and lead it out of slavery.

The faith, righteousness, and prompt obedience of Joseph together with Mary are part of God's transcendent purpose.

Possible Personal Applications

The angel who announced to Joseph his vocation now appears again to him in this time of crisis.

Jesus' father is to save the Savior, fleeing with Jesus and Mary on a moment's notice as refugees in a foreign land. Joseph humbly exercises his role as head of the Holy Family in a spirit of service to Jesus and Mary, whom he recognizes as greatly superior to himself. He will sacrifice anything for them. He obeys unquestioningly and without hesitation. Without complaint or hesitation Mary trusts his word and follows his lead, gratefully recognizing that God chose Joseph to fulfill this role for them. The Holy Spouses share the deep pain of realizing that the earthly powers want to kill the Giver of life whom they treasure with all their hearts. However, they also share and reinforce each other in their trust that divine providence will always accompany their efforts. They immediately launch out into the fearful unknown, in the assurance that God is with them.

The terrible suffering of the Holy Family is the vehicle for much greater joy and blessings. Ancient tradition reports that, at the presence of the God-child, Egyptian idols tumbled to the ground in Hermopolis Magna thus fulfilling Isaiah 19:1: "the Lord ... comes to Egypt; and the idols of Egypt will tremble at his presence."[52] Herod died, and again through Joseph the angel of God calls his Son out of Egypt to return to the promised land to establish the new covenant. All that the Holy Spouses endured only led them to marvel ever more deeply at God's amazing work being accomplished in their home.

We pray for fathers of families to lead their families in prayerfully listening to God and obeying his will. We pray for all parents to protect their children from current spiritual threats that are even more dangerous than Herod's wicked intention. We pray that immigrants, refugees, the homeless, the unemployed, travelers, missionaries, and all who suffer may always persevere in the trust that God's providence will not fail them.

Dear Mary and Joseph, pray that suffering or difficulty may never deter us from fleeing temptation in prompt obedience to God's will, and that we may always trust that every cross embraced brings new life, because "God makes all things work together for the good of those who love Him" (Rom 8:28).

Contemplate

With the Holy Spouses first puzzle at the mystery of God Incarnate become dependent, threatened, a refugee with a price on his head. Then contemplate God's providence using this suffering to come to replace pagan idolatry and then return to the promised land as the true King of the New Covenant to which we are blessed to belong.

The *Our Father*

Meditative Tenfold Repetition of the *Holy Spouses Prayer*

Mary, full of grace, and Joseph, son of David; honor to you, Mother of God, and to you, guardian of the Redeemer. Eternal praise to the child with whom you formed a family, JESUS, OUR KING.

Holy Spouses, pray for us sinners, our families and communities, now and at the hour of our death. Amen.

The Glory Be

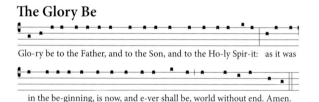

Glo-ry be to the Father, and to the Son, and to the Ho-ly Spir-it: as it was

in the be-ginning, is now, and e-ver shall be, world without end. Amen.

Invocation to St. Joseph Marello

St. Joseph Marello,
pray for us.

THE NINTH MYSTERY OF THE INCARNATION AND HIDDEN LIFE

The Finding of Jesus in the Temple

At the age of twelve Jesus stays behind in the temple, amazing the teachers by his understanding. His parents, Joseph and Mary, first are anguished at his being lost and then are confronted with the mystery of Jesus' reference to the temple as his "Father's house."

Listen to the Word of God

Now his parents went to Jerusalem every year at the feast of the Passover. And when he was twelve years old, they went up according to custom; and when the feast was ended, as they were returning, the boy Jesus stayed behind in Jerusalem. His parents did not know it, but supposing him to be in the company they went a day's journey, and they sought him among their kinsfolk and acquaintances; and

*when they did not find him, they returned
to Jerusalem, seeking him. After three
days they found him in the temple, sitting
among the teachers, listening to them and
asking them questions; and all who heard
him were amazed at his understanding
and his answers. And when they saw him
they were astonished; and his mother said
to him, "Son, why have you treated us so?
Behold, your father and I have been looking for you anxiously." And he said to them,
"How is it that you sought me? Did you not
know that I must be in my Father's house?"
And they did not understand the saying
which he spoke to them* (Lk 2:41-50).

The Biblical Background

This passage is the only one in the Gospels that
relates anything of the intervening years between
Jesus' infancy and the beginning of his public
ministry as an adult. In Luke it provides a transi-
tion from childhood since it is integrally related
with the preceding passage regarding the presentation of the child. Mary and Joseph had offered
him completely to God in the temple soon after
birth. When Jesus is twelve he is of age to make
that offering his own. He is not lost, but decides for
himself to stay behind in the temple. Aware now of
his mission, he already shows a willingness to offer

himself completely to God. This offering will be consummated on the cross.

Realizing that the will of his heavenly Father takes precedence over human parental ties, Jesus does not inform Joseph and Mary that he is staying behind. After a day's journey they are anguished at the awareness of being separated from him for the first time. They return to Jerusalem to look for him. On the third day they find him interacting with the teachers in the temple. Their relief at finding him is mingled with amazement at his answers and their astonishment that he had stayed without telling them. Mary speaks on behalf of Joseph and herself. The Holy Spouses have been searching anxiously. She mentions his father first, according to the hierarchy of family authority. Their astonishment is matched by his. Why were they seeking him? Did they not know that he had to be in his Father's house? Mary and Joseph hear him refer not to Joseph, his earthly father, but to God, his heavenly Father. They witness the mystery beyond human understanding: their Son's self-offering to God will involve the loss of separation and the sword of sorrows prophesied by Simeon.

Possible Personal Applications

Despite their deep anguish at their separation from Jesus, the Holy Spouses do not react to Jesus with anger or severity, but only with heartfelt questioning, in search of an explanation. They speak as a united couple to their twelve-year-old Son. Joseph shows Mary deference by allowing her to do the talking, while she shows him deference by mentioning him as father first when addressing their Son. All parents are called to imitate the unity and respect of the Holy Spouses in dealing with their children, especially during adolescence when new challenges and adjustments take place in the parent-child dynamic.

In their anxiety Mary and Joseph spontaneously knew to look for Jesus in the temple. On finding him conversing on a par with the doctors, they are also filled with a sense of holy wonder. Their little helpless baby has so quickly become a young man already showing divine wisdom. Their question about why he did not ask or even inform them fades into the background, in light of the realization that he is already looking toward the fulfilment of his divine mission. They were not ready for this as Jesus had expected them to be, but they listen respectfully as they seek to understand what their role is to be as Jesus will set out on his own to do his Father's business. Neither Joseph nor Mary questions the fact that God is the one Father and that their parenthood is always subservient to God's. Jesus is only following what they have taught him: he belongs to God and is to fulfill the mission given him by his heavenly Father. All parental authority is under God's authority and is to be exercised in union with it. Parents are to help children find and follow their vocation in life. While always maintaining respect for his or her parents, every child is to grow to seek and respond to the plan of the heavenly Father in life, whether it be an eventual call to marriage or to consecrated virginity for the sake of the kingdom.

The challenging event described in this mystery is also filled with beauty. Previously known to Mary and Joseph only through faith, the mystery of the Incarnation now begins to develop in the words and actions of the One Incarnate. The Holy Family grows together even more in this new stage of their journey, a model for every family.

We pray for faith, unity, understanding, and healing for all parents and adolescent children, especially those experiencing family tensions, misunderstandings, barriers, or alienation during this period. We pray that families may be the cradle of the Church, the seed-bed where the future vocations to marriage, priesthood, and religious life are nurtured. We pray for youth to hear God's call amidst the world's noisy distractions.

Dear Mary and Joseph, pray that our concerns or plans may never interfere or compete with those of God. May we always seek and help others seek above all to be in the Father's house and to do the Father's will.

Contemplate

With the Holy Spouses stand in amazement at the twelve-year-old Jesus as he manifests divine wisdom while conversing with the religious teachers. Contemplate the mystery of the same Son of God present still in our Church, his Father's house, teaching us all Truth.

The *Our Father*

Meditative Tenfold Repetition of the *Holy Spouses Prayer*

Mary, full of grace, and Joseph, son of David; honor to you, Mother of God, and to you, guardian of the Redeemer. Eternal praise to the child with whom you formed a family, JESUS, SON OF GOD.

Holy Spouses, pray for us sinners, our families and communities, now and at the hour of our death. Amen.

The Glory Be

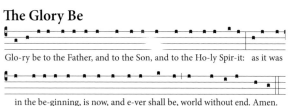

Glo-ry be to the Father, and to the Son, and to the Ho-ly Spir-it: as it was

in the be-ginning, is now, and e-ver shall be, world without end. Amen.

Invocation to St. Joseph Marello

St. Joseph Marello,
pray for us.

THE TENTH MYSTERY OF THE INCARNATION AND HIDDEN LIFE

The Hidden Life at Nazareth

The Incarnate Son of God for thirty years lives obedient to his parents in an ordinary, hidden life of prayer, family, and work, before beginning his public ministry. Mary and Joseph secretly ponder and guard the mystery of God sanctifying our everyday lives an ' calling us to holiness in the ordinary.

Listen to the Word of God

And he went down with them and came to Nazareth, and was obedient to them; and his mother kept all these things in her heart. And Jesus increased in wisdom and in stature, and in favor with God and man (Lk 2:51-52).

Jesus, when he began his ministry, was about thirty years of age, being the son (as was supposed) of Joseph (Lk 3:23).

The Biblical Background

After the episode at the temple when Jesus was twelve, he returned with Joseph and Mary "to Nazareth," his home town (Lk 1:26; 2:4, 39). We hear no more about him in the Scriptures until he begins his public ministry at the age of thirty. When he then returns to preach in the Nazareth synagogue, his own townsfolk reject him. They are unable to believe that he could be the anointed one prophesied by Isaiah, because they find him too ordinary (Lk 4:16-29). From the other Gospels we also learn that the chosen people in general had trouble believing that anything good could come from Nazareth (Jn 1:46). No prophet is foretold from Galilee (Jn 7:41-42, 52). Matthew has to convince his Jewish readers to overcome this scandal of Nazareth and realize that the prophecies are fulfilled in ways they never imagined by Jesus being known as a Nazarene (2:23).

Jesus remained "obedient to" his parents in the ongoing mystery of the hidden life at Nazareth. The Son of God Incarnate learned from them and grew "in wisdom and in stature, and in favor with God and man." Ordinary family life in an ordinary town of no particular significance constitutes thirty of the thirty-three years of Jesus' earthly existence. Obedience in a family during this time expresses obedience to the will of the Father, that will ultimately be consummated on the cross (Phlp 2:8).

Mary appears alone throughout Jesus' public ministry, at the foot of his cross, and with the apostles when the Church is born at Pentecost. Joseph is not heard of, leading to the conclusion that he must have died. By the time of Jesus' public ministry Joseph has completed his role as earthly father to him, naming, nurturing, protecting, and educating him in the faith and in the profession of carpentry. From good Joseph's faithful care, the child learned by human experience that no earthly father would give his son a serpent instead of a fish, or a scorpion instead of an egg. Jesus' revelation to us, however, is how much more the heavenly Father in his infinite goodness will give us the Holy Spirit (Lk 11:11-13). His human identity as "son of Joseph" causes confusion for Jesus' proclamation that he is Son of God (Mt 13:55; Jn 6:42).

Even after the Incarnation the "mystery hidden for ages" (Eph 3:9; Col 1:26) remained hidden for the thirty years at Nazareth. Through our Baptism into Christ that mystery remains hidden in us in a life that transcends this visible flesh (Col 3:3).

Possible Personal Applications

The mystery of the hidden life of the Holy Family at Nazareth testifies that we are all called to holiness in our everyday lives. It is not what attracts the world's attention that counts. It matters little how famous we are, how wealthy, or how successful. What ultimately matters is how holy we are, how close to Christ we live each day. The Holy Spouses teach us to ponder in our hearts daily the mystery of Christ present in our midst, in the simplest, most ordinary circumstances and events. Little, unnoticed deeds done out of love for God and others bear tremendous value for eternity.

Family life is a vocation taking precedence over career. The love of husband and wife images the unity of the three Divine Persons in the Holy Trinity. All husbands and wives are called to be holy spouses. As parents together they share in the noble calling of raising children and forming holy families with them. Their parenting is to image God the Father, and is to recall always with humility that human parents are instruments of his ultimate authority. Parents help children follow their God-given vocation, while still guiding them until the proper time for them to set out on their own. Children, especially teenagers, draw inspiration from the Son of God to be obedient, even when strongly pulled in contrary directions.

Those called to states of virginity draw special inspiration from the virginal love of Jesus, Mary, and Joseph. Chastity freely embraced for the kingdom has the power to open lives to greater love of God and neighbor. Apparent barrenness may produce abundant fruit for eternity. Consecrated virginity is a sign of the future wedding feast of the Lamb.

Work is not an end in itself, not simply a means to a salary or prestige, but an expression of love, a means for glorifying God and putting one's gifts at the service of others.

St. Joseph's presumed death in the arms of Jesus and Mary[53] leads us all to ask the Holy Spouses to intercede for us "now and at the hour of our death," so that we may found united with Jesus so as also to enter eternal glory.

Dear Mary and Joseph, pray for us to be purified from all vainglory and self-importance, in a life of obedience to the will of the Father especially in the little matters of each moment. Help us to live "hidden with Christ in God," doing the ordinary with extraordinary love.

Contemplate

Peacefully visualize the Holy Family at Nazareth, working, praying, studying, eating, conversing, laughing. Imagine how amidst the various events taking place throughout their years, the Holy Spouses always have Jesus at the center of their lives. Experience Jesus, Mary, and Joseph calling you to holiness in your ordinary, everyday life.

The *Our Father*

Meditative Tenfold Repetition of the
Holy Spouses Prayer

Mary, full of grace, and Joseph, son of David; honor to you, Mother of God, and to you, guardian of the Redeemer. Eternal praise to the child with whom you formed a family, JESUS, OBEDIENT UNTO DEATH.

Holy Spouses, pray for us sinners, our families and communities, now and at the hour of our death. Amen.

The Glory Be

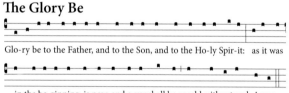

Glo-ry be to the Father, and to the Son, and to the Ho-ly Spir-it: as it was

in the be-ginning, is now, and e-ver shall be, world without end. Amen.

Invocation to St. Joseph Marello

St. Joseph Marello,
pray for us.

Concluding Prayers

Hail, Holy Queen

Hail, holy Queen, mother of mercy, our life, our sweetness and our hope. To thee do we cry, poor banished children of Eve. To thee do we send up our sighs, mourning and weeping in this valley of tears. Turn then, most gracious advocate, thine eyes of mercy toward us, and after this our exile, show unto us the blessed fruit of thy womb, Jesus. O clement, O loving, O sweet Virgin Mary.

Prayer of Pope Leo XIII to St. Joseph

To you, O Blessed Joseph, we come in our trials, and having asked the help of your most holy spouse, we confidently ask your patronage also. Through that sacred bond of charity which united you to the Immaculate Virgin Mother of God and through the fatherly love with which you embraced the child Jesus, we humbly beg you to look graciously upon the beloved inheritance which Jesus Christ purchased by his blood, and to aid us in our necessities with your power and strength.

O most provident guardian of the Holy Family, defend the chosen children of Jesus Christ. Most beloved father, dispel the evil of falsehood and sin. Our most mighty protector, graciously assist us from heaven in our struggle with the powers of darkness. And just as you once saved the Child Jesus from mortal danger, so now defend God's Holy Church from the snares of her enemies and from all adversity. Shield each one of us by your constant protection, so that, supported by your example and your help, we may be able to live a virtuous life, to die a holy death, and to obtain eternal happiness in heaven. Amen.

Holy Spouses Litany

Lord, have mercy	Lord, have mercy
Christ, have mercy	Christ, have mercy
Lord, have mercy	Lord, have mercy
God our Father in heaven	have mercy on us
God the Son, Redeemer of the world	
	have mercy on us
God the Holy Spirit	have mercy on us
Holy Trinity, one God	have mercy on us
Holy Mary	pray for us
Saint Joseph	pray for us
Holy Spouses	pray for us

Holy parents of Jesus	pray for us
Holy protectors of the Body of Christ	pray for us
Teachers of the Holy Child	pray for us
Holy Virgins	pray for us
Spouses most loving	pray for us
Spouses most faithful	pray for us
Spouses most pure	pray for us
Spouses most just	pray for us
Spouses most obedient	pray for us
Spouses most humble	pray for us
Spouses most generous	pray for us
Models of family life	pray for us
Models for couples	pray for us
Models of parenthood	pray for us
Parents to those without parents	pray for us
Patrons of the unborn	pray for us
Models for virgins	pray for us
Lovers of poverty	pray for us
Comfort of the troubled	pray for us
Servants of the Lord	pray for us
Ministers of Salvation	pray for us
Mother and Patron of the Church	pray for us

Lamb of God, who takes away the sins of the world
spare us, O Lord

Lamb of God, who takes away the sins of the world
hear us, O Lord

Lamb of God, who takes away the sins of the world
have mercy on us

Holy Father, who joined together by a virginal bond the glorious Mother of your Son and the just man, Saint Joseph, that they might be faithful cooperators in the mystery of the Word Incarnate, we beseech you, that by meditating upon the mysteries of the Incarnation and hidden life of your only begotten Son, we may live in more intimate union with Christ and may walk more joyfully in the way of love, through the same Christ our Lord. Amen.

The Sign of the Cross

In the name of the Father, and of the Son, and of the Holy Spirit. Amen.

Final Praise

Praised be Jesus Christ!
Now and forever. Amen.

The Holy Spouses Rosary in Various Languages

Lingua Latina

Maria, gratia plena, et Ioseph, fili David, laus vobis, Dei Matri et Redemptoris custodi. Eterna gloria pueri quocum formavistis familiam, IESU.

Sancti Coniuges, orate pro nobis peccatoribus, pro familiis et communitatibus nostris, nunc et in hora mortis nostrae. Amen.

Misteria Incarnationis et Vitae Absconditae

1. Maria desponsata Ioseph (Mt 1:18a; Lc 1:26-27; 2:4-5a).
2. Angelus nuntiat Mariae (Lc 1:28-38).
3. Angelus nuntiat Ioseph (Mt 1:18b-23).
4. Ioseph accipit coniugem suam (Mt 1:24-25).
5. Puer natus est Iesus (Lc 2:6-16).
6. Circumcisio et Nomen Iesu (Lc 2:21).
7. Sistunt eum in Templo (Lc 2:22-35).
8. Fuga et vocatio ex Aegypto (Mt 2:13-15).
9. Inveniunt eum in Templo (Lc 2:41-50).
10. Vita abscondita Nazareth (Lc 2:51-52).

Italiano

Maria, piena di grazia, e Giuseppe, figlio di Davide: onore a te, Madre di Dio, e a te, Custode del Redentore. Lode eterna al Figlio, col Quale avete formato una famiglia, GESÙ.

Santi Sposi, pregate per noi peccatori, per le nostre famiglie e comunità, adesso e nell'ora della nostra morte. Amen.

I Misteri dell'Incarnazione e della Vita Nascosta

1. Maria era promessa sposa di Giuseppe (Mt 1,18a; Lc 1,26-27; 2,4-5a).
2. Annunciazione di Maria (Lc 1,28-38).
3. Annunciazione di Giuseppe (Mt 1,18b-23).
4. Giuseppe riceve nella sua casa Maria come sua sposa (Mt 1,24-25).
5. Gesù nasce in Betlemme (Lc 2, 6-16).
6. Circoncisione e imposizione del nome di Gesù (Lc 2,21).
7. Presentazione di Gesù nel Tempio (Lc 2,22-35).
8. Fuga e Ritorno da Egitto (Mt 2,13-15).
9. Ritrovamento di Gesù nel Tempio (Lc 2,41-50).
10. Vita nascosta a Nazaret (Lc 2,51-52).

Español (Latinoamericano)

María, llena de gracia, y José, hijo de David; honor a ti, Madre de Dios, y a ti, custodio del Redentor. Eterna alabanza al Niño con quien formaron una familia, Jesús.

Santos Esposos, rueguen por nosotros pecadores, por nuestras familias y comunidades, ahora y en la hora de nuestra muerte. Amén.

Los Misterios de la Encarnación y la Vida Escondida
1. Los desposorios de María y José (Mt 1,18a; Lc 1,26-27; 2,4-5a).
2. El anuncio del ángel a María (Lc 1,28-38).
3. El anuncio del ángel a José (Mt 1,18b-23).
4. José recibió en su casa a su esposa (Mt 1,24-25).
5. El nacimiento del Niño Jesús (Lc 2, 6-16).
6. La circuncisión y el Nombre de Jesús (Lc 2,21).
7. La presentación en el templo (Lc 2,22-35).
8. La huida y el regreso de Egipto (Mt 2,13-15).
9. El joven Jesús hallado en el templo (Lc 2,41-50).
10. La vida escondida en Nazaret (Lc 2,51-52).

Português (Brasileiro)

Maria, cheia de graça, e José, filho de Davi; honra a você, Mãe de Deus, e a você, guardião do Redentor. Eterno louvor à criança com a qual vocês formaram a família, JESUS.

Santos Esposos, rogai por nós pecadores, por nossas famílias e comunidades, agora e na hora de nossa morte. Amém.

Os Mistérios da Encarnação e da Vida Escondida

1. O Desposório de Maria e José (Mt 1:18a, Lc 1:26-27, 2:4-5a).
2. A Anunciação à Maria (Lc 1:28-38).
3. A Anunciação a José (Mt 1:18b-23).
4. José recebe em sua casa Maria sua esposa (Mt 1:24-25).
5. O Nascimento de Jesus (Lc 2:6-16).
6. A Circuncisão e o Nome de Jesus (Lc 2:21).
7. A Apresentação de Jesus (Lc 2:22-35).
8. A Fuga e a volta do Egito (Mt 2:13-15).
9. O jovem Jesus no Templo (Lc 2:41-50).
10. A Vida escondida em Nazaré (Lc 2:51-52).

Polski

Maryjo, łaski pełna, i Józefie, synu Dawida; wszelka cześć tobie, Matko Boża, i tobie, opiekunie Zbawiciela. Niech będzie uwielbione na wieki dzieciątko z którym utworzyliście rodzinę, JEZUS.

Święci Małżonkowie, módlcie się za nami grzesznymi, za nasze rodziny i wspólnoty, teraz i w godzinę śmierci naszej. Amen.

Tajemnice Wcielenia i Życia Ukrytego

1. Zaślubiny Maryi i Józefa (Mt 1:18a, Łk 1:26-27, 2:4-5a).
2. Zwiastowanie Maryi (Łk 1:28-38).
3. Zwiastowanie Józefowi (Mt 1:18b-23).
4. Józef bierze do siebie Maryję (Mt 1:24-25).
5. Narodzenie Jezusa (Łk 2:6-16).
6. Obrzezanie i nadanie imienia Jezusowi (Łk 2:21).
7. Ofiarowanie Jezusa w świątyni (Łk 2:22-40).
8. Ucieczka do Egiptu i powrót z ziemi egipskiej (Mt 2:13-15).
9. Odnalezienie Jezusa w świątyni (Łk 2:41-50).
10. Ukryte życie w Nazarecie (Łk 2:51-52, 3:23).

Filipino (Tagalog)

María, napúpuno ka ng grasya, at José, anák ni David; ipinagdárangal namin kayo, Iná ng Diyós, at taga-pag-alaga ng Manunubos. Kasama sa Banál na Mag-anak papuri magpakáylanman sa inyong Anák na si JESÚS.

Banál na Mag-asawa, ipanalangin ninyo kamíng makasalanan, ang aming mga pamilya at pámayanan, ngayón at kung kamí'y mamámatay. Amén.

Ang Mga Misteryo ng Pagkakatawang-táo at Tagóng-buhay

1. Ang Kásunduang Pagpapakasal (Mt 1:18a; Lc 1:26-27. 2:4-5a)
2. Ang Pagbabalita kay María (Lc 1:28-38)
3. Ang Pagbabalita kay José (Mt 1:18b-23)
4. Tinanggáp ni José si María Bilang Asawa (Mt 1:24-25)
5. Ang Kapanganakan ni Jesús (Lc 2:6-16)
6. Ang Pagtutuli at Pagpapangalan kay Jesús (Lc 2:21)
7. Ang Pagdádala kay Jesús sa Templo (Lc 2:22-35)
8. Ang Pagtakas patungong Ehipto at ang Pagbábalik (Mt 2:13-15)
9. Ang Pagkakita kay Jesús sa Templo (Lc 2:41-50)
10. Ang Tagóng-buhay sa Nazarét (Lc 2:51-52. 3:23)

Malayalam

നന്മ നിറഞ്ഞ മറിയമേ, ദാവീദിന്റെ പുത്രനായ യൗസേപ്പേ, ദൈവ മാതാവായ അങ്ങേക്കും രക്ഷകന്റെ വളർത്തുപിതാവായ അങ്ങേക്കും സ്തുതി. നിങ്ങളുടെ കുടുംബാംഗമായ ഈശോയ്ക്ക് നിത്യവും സ്തുതിയും പുകഴ്ചയുമുണ്ടായിരിക്കട്ടെ.

വിശുദ്ധ ദമ്പതിമാരെ, പാപികളായ ഞങ്ങൾക്കുവേണ്ടിയും ഞങ്ങളുടെ കുടുംബങ്ങൾക്കുവേണ്ടിയും സമൂഹങ്ങൾക്കു വേണ്ടിയും ഇപ്പോഴും ഞങ്ങളുടെ മരണ സമയത്തും പ്രാർത്ഥിക്കണമേ. ആമേൻ.

മനുഷ്യാവതാരത്തിന്റെയും നസറത്തു ജീവിതത്തിന്റെയും രഹസ്യങ്ങൾ

1. വിവാഹ നിശ്ചയം [മറിയവും യൗസേപ്പും തമ്മിലുള്ള വിവാഹ ന
   ിശ്ചയം] (മത്താ 1:18; ലൂക്കാ 1:26-27; 2:4-5)
2. മറിയത്തിനു ലഭിച്ച മംഗളവാർത്ത (ലൂക്കാ 1:28-38)
3. യൗസേപ്പിനു ലഭിച്ച മംഗളവാർത്ത (മത്താ 1:18-23)
4. യൗസേപ്പ് തന്റെ ഭാര്യയായ മറിയത്തെ സ്വഭവനത്തിൽ
   സ്വീകരിക്കുന്നു (മത്താ 1:24-25)
5. യേശുവിന്റെ ജനനം (ലൂക്കാ 2:6-16)
6. യേശുവിന്റെ രിഛേദനകർമ്മവും നാമകരണവും (ലൂക്കാ 2:21)
7. യേശുവിന്റെ സമർപ്പണം (ലൂക്കാ 2:22-35)
8. ഈജിപ്തിലേക്കുള്ള പാലായനവും തിരിച്ചുവരവും (മത്താ
   2:13-15)
9. യേശുവിനെ ദേവാലയത്തിൽ കണ്ടെത്തുന്നു (ലൂക്കാ 2:41-50)
10. നസറത്തിലെ രഹസ്യ ജീവിതം (ലൂക്കാ 2:51-52; 3:23)

Igbo

Maria juputara n'amara, na Josef nwa David; ugwu diri gi nne nke Chukwu, na gi onye nchedo onye Nzoputa. Otito ebighiebi diri nwa ahu sonyere n'ezi n'ulo unu bu JESU.

Di na nwunye di aso, riobara anyi bu ndi njo ariro, ezi n'ulo anyi na obodo anyi, kita na amano onwu anyi Amen.

Ihe Omimi Nke Iwere Ahu Na Ndu Nzizo Nke Jesu

1. Nkwekorita ilu Maria di Aso (Mt 1:18a, Lk 1:26-27, 2:4-5a).
2. Ikwuputere Maria maka imu Jesu (Lk 1:28-38).
3. Ikwuputere Josef maka ime nke nwunye ya Maria (Mt 1:18b-23).
4. Josef ikpobanye Maria nwunye ya n'ulo ya (Mt 1:24-25).
5. Omumu nke Jesu (Lk 2:6-16).
6. Obibi ugwu na igu afa nke Jesu (Lk 2:21).
7. Nkuputa nke Jesu n'ulo uka (Lk 2:22-35).
8. Mgbaga na nloghachita azu site n'ala Ejiptu (Mt 2:13-15).
9. Ichota Jesu n'ulo uka (Lk 2:41-50).
10. Ndu nzizo n'ala Nazaret (Lk 2:51-52; 3:23).

Endnotes

1. *Quamquam Pluries*, 8/15/1889. See "Concluding Prayers," page 101.

2. *Redemptoris Custos (RC)*, 8/15/1989, 31.

3. *Rosarium Virginis Mariae (RVM)*, 10/16/2002, 6.

4. *RVM*, 15, 25.

5. *RVM*, 1.

6. Cf. *RVM*, 10.

7. *RVM*, 12.

8. *RVM*, 14.

9. Blessed Bartolo Longo, *The Fifteen Saturdays of the Most Holy Rosary*, quoted in *RVM*, 15.

10. *RVM*, 15-16. *RC*, 28.

11. *RC*, 7.

12. Cf. *RC*, 17-18, 28.

13. *Catechism of the Catholic Church (CCC)*, 517, and generally 512-534.

14. *RC*.

15. *RVM*, 2, 18.

16. *CCC*, 515.

17. *CCC*, 516.

18. *CCC*, 517, 522.

19. Buccellati, Giorgio, "The Prophetic Dimension of Joseph," *Communio* 33 (Spring 2006), pp. 43-99.

20. Lc 3:23; 4:22; Mt 13:55; Jn 1:45; 6:42.

21. *RVM*, 18.

22. *RC*, 18.

23. *YOUCAT, Youth Catechism of the Catholic Church* (2011), 86.

24. *RVM*, 38.

25. *Oblates of St. Joseph Proper Mass Texts*, 1997, pp. 7-15, Guardian of the Redeemer Publications, 544 W. Cliff Dr., Santa Cruz, CA 95060-6147; 1-(866)-MARELLO; www.osjoseph.org.

26. *RVM*, Chapter III.

27. *RVM*, 32.

28. Rom 8:15; Gal 4:6.

29. *RVM*, 33.

30. Cf. Acts 4:12; Phlp 2:9-11.

31. *Marialis Cultus*, 2/2/1974, 46. Also Congregation for Divine Worship, *Directory on Popular Piety and the Liturgy*, 12/17/2001, 201.

32. *RVM*, 34.

33. Preaching at Milliavacca Institute, beginning 10/8/1881, quoted in Toschi, *Saint Joseph in the Life of Two Blesseds of the Church*, 97, pp. 79-80. This and other literature on St. Marello is available from Guardian of the Redeemer Publications, referenced above in note 25. Cf. particularly, *Holiness in the Ordinary*, 1993.

34. *RVM*, 5.

35. *RVM*, 41-42.

36. Cf. Toschi, "St. Joseph, Model of Love and Life," in *St. Joseph Studies*, Santa Cruz, CA, Guardian of the Redeemer, 2002, pp. 143-158.

37. See also *Family of St. Joseph Prayer Manual*, Santa Cruz, CA, Guardian of the Redeemer, for the eightfold commitment of couples in the "Holy Spouse Society," as well as the rite of enrollment in this spiritual society, and the rite of enthronement of the Holy Spouses Image in one's home.

38. Cf. Toschi, *Joseph in the New Testament*, Santa Cruz, CA, Guardian of the Redeemer, 1991, pp. 23-27.

39. 2 Sam 7:11-14; cf. Ps 89:20-38; Ps 132; Acts 2:30-31.

40. *CCC*, 490-493.

41. Letter 212 [185] to the Oblates of St. Joseph, Acqui, 3/25/1890, Feast of the Annunciation to Mary.

42. Cf. Toschi, *Joseph in the New Testament*, pp. 23-36; Buccellati, *op. cit.*

43. In Matthew 28:20, for example, Jesus' promise to remain with his disciples *until* the end of the age does not imply that he will not be with them afterwards. In 2 Samuel 6:23 (2 Kings 6:23 in the Greek Old Testament), the fact that Michal had no children *until* the day of her death, certainly does not imply that she had any after death. Church Tradition always understood that the "brothers of the Lord" were not biological sons of Mary and Joseph, but rather cousins or other relatives, in accord with the broad meaning of the biblical word for "brother," as seen for example in Genesis 13:8, where the

word is applied to Abraham and Lot, who are uncle and nephew.

44. *RC*, 9.

45. Undated counsel to Sr. Albertina Fasolis, quoted in Toschi, *Saint Joseph in the Life of Two Blesseds*, p. 78.

46. Cf. Toschi, "The Mystery of the Circumcision and Naming of Jesus," in *Saint Joseph, Patron for our Times, Proceedings of the Tenth International Josephological Congress*, Centrum Józefologiczne, Kalisz, Poland, 2010, pp. 121-135; "El Misterio de la circuncisión y el deber del padre de dar el nombre," in *San José, Custodio de las Familias, Conferencias Congreso Nacional*, Oblatos de San José, Monterrey, NL, México, 2011, pp. 54-67.

47. Cf. Dt 30:6; Jer 31:31; Rom 15:8; Heb 9:15, 12:24.

48. Cf. Lk 22:30; Col 2:11-12; *CCC*, 527.

49. Cf. Toschi, "Joseph and Egypt," in *Die Bedeutung des hl. Josef in der Heilsgeschichte, Akten des IX. Internationalen Symposions über den heiligen Josef*, Internationalen Mariologischen Arbeitskreises Kevelaer (IMAK), Kevelaer, Germany, 2006, pp. 277-299.

50. The association of Joseph and Egypt at the beginning of the New Testament also recalls the Old Testament Joseph, son of the patriarch, Jacob-Israel. He was also a "man of dreams." He had been sold into slavery in Egypt, but ended up winning favor and saving his people from famine. See Genesis, chapters 37-50.

51. Cf. Jer 31:31-4; Heb 8:8-13.

52. Cf. also Jer 43:12-13; Ez 20:7-8; 30:13.

53. Cf. Toschi, et al. *Husband, Worker, Father*, Ch. 8 "Joseph's Death," Liguori, MO, 2012, pp. 57-60.

Graphic credits

Front cover, Fr. Franco Verri, C.S.J., 1989, Oblates of St. Joseph, Asti, Italy;

Rosary, music for the Glory be, cover, and layout, Fr. Matthew Spencer, O.S.J.;

Mysteries: 1) Gandolfino da Roreto, 1505, Asti Cathedral;

2) St. Patrick Basilica, Montreal, Canada;

3) Mario Caffaro Rore, Italy;

4) Fr. Verri, 1991;

5) St. Patrick Parish, Omaha, NE;

6) Perdriau and O'Shea workshop, 1919, Oratoire Saint-Joseph, Montreal;

7) Cathedral of Los Ángeles, CA;

8) St. Joseph Parish, Garrett, IN;

9) St. Joseph Parish, Omaha;

10) Cathedral of Cologne, Germany.

Photographs of mysteries 1-2 and 5-10 and on back cover by Fr. Toschi.

The Oblates of St. Joseph

The Congregation of the Oblates of Saint Joseph was founded on March 14, 1878 by St. Joseph Marello in northwestern Italy, in the city of Asti. Initially, it gathered young men who desired to consecrate themselves privately to the love and service of Jesus in imitation of St. Joseph. Eventually, as understood by divine providence, it took the form of a religious congregation of priests and brothers taking the vows of chastity, poverty and obedience with official recognition by the local and universal Church.

The Oblates of St. Joseph live in fraternal community and seek to serve Christ and His Church primarily by spreading devotion to St. Joseph, Christian formation of youth, and assisting the local churches by providing pastoral work in areas of great need and suffering. The Oblates of Saint Joseph have engaged the laity in places where they work by inviting them to share in their spiritual and pastoral endeavors. The "spiritual sons of St. Joseph Marello" can be found serving the Church in 13 different countries throughout the world, including the United States, particularly in Pennsylvania and California. After working for many decades as two separate provinces, they have now recently merged into one unified province and placed under the patronage and protection of the *Holy Spouses.*

The vision of St. Joseph Marello continues to live strongly today in various cultures, countries, and languages. His life of holiness and tireless dedication to the Church was recognized by the Universal Church as worthy of imitation when he was canonized a saint by Blessed John Paul II in 2001.

The Oblates of St. Joseph religious family welcomes any young man who wishes to totally serve the Divine Master through the faithful living of the evangelical counsels. Kindly include within your daily prayer intentions an increase of holy vocations to the Church, especially to the Oblates of St. Joseph.

Rev. Paul A. McDonnell, O.S.J.
Provincial Superior, *Holy Spouses Province*

March 14, 2013, date of U. S. A. province unification and 135th anniversary of the founding of the Oblates of St. Joseph in Italy.

Other Materials Available

The Holy Spouses Rosary Leaflet, 8-panel color pocket-size leaflet. Also available in Spanish.

Guardian of the Redeemer Magazine, quarterly 32 page periodical on St. Joseph according to the spirituality of the Oblates of St. Joseph.

St. Joseph, Guardian of the Redeemer, Text and Reflections, by Pope John Paul II and Fr. Tarcisio Stramare, O.S.J., 160 pages.

Joseph in the New Testament, by Fr. Toschi, 156 pages.

St. Joseph Studies, Symposia papers, 171 pages.

Husband, Father, Worker, by Fr. Toschi, 128 pages.

Joseph: The Man Closest to Christ, 60 minute DVD.

Guardian of the Redeemer Publications
544 W. Cliff Dr., Santa Cruz, CA   95060-6147
1 (866) MARELLO
guardian@osjoseph.org
www.osjoseph.org

Guardian of the Redeemer Publications
544 West Cliff Dr.
Santa Cruz, CA 95060

http://osjoseph.org